A CLASSROOM PRESENTS

THE CONSTITUTION OF
THE UNITED STATES

A Story for Elementary School Children

Written and Illustrated by Janice Howes, M.Ed.

TEACHERS PUBLISHING HOUSE
P. O. Box 9358
Canton, Ohio 44711

I would like to thank the following people for the time they spent in reviewing this book, and for their many helpful suggestions, criticisms, and encouraging comments:

Walter E. Arms, Ph.D.
Elementary Education Dept.
University of Akron
Akron, Ohio

Loran Braught, Ph.D.
School of Education
Indiana State University

Guy Clifford, Ph.D.
Dept. of Political Science
Bridgewater State College
Bridgewater, Massachusetts

James Dague, Ph.D.
Dept. of Education
John Carroll University
Cleveland, Ohio

Gloria Fimbres, Ph.D.
Teacher Education Program
University of California
San Diego, California

Arlene F. Gallagher, Ph.D.
School of Education
Boston University

Linda Gromer
Dir. of Instructional Media
Kentwood Public Schools
Kentwood, Michigan

William W. Joyce, Ph.D.
Professor of Education
Michigan State University

Ronald Kirkemo, Ph.D.
Professor, Political Science
Point Loma Nazarene College
San Diego, California

Kelly Koelker
Attorney
Atlanta, Georgia

Tarry L. Lindquist
Elementary Teacher
Mercer Island School District
Mercer Island, Washington

David Mancini, Ph.D.
Curriculum Director
Louisville Public Schools
Louisville, Ohio

James Martin
Social Studies Consultant
Stark County Dept. of Education
Louisville, Ohio

Maryanne Metcalfe, M.A., M.Ed.
English Department
Kent State University
Canton, Ohio

Karen O'Connor
Author
San Diego, California

Walter C. Parker, Ph.D.
College of Education
University of Washington
Seattle, Washington

Michael E. Parrish, Ph.D.
Dept. of History
University of California
San Diego, California

John Patrick, Ph.D.
Director, Soc. Studies Dev. Center
Indiana University

Richard C. Remy, Ph.D.
Director, Citizenship Dev. Program
Mershon Center
The Ohio State University

David E. Ross
History Teacher
Plain Local Schools
Canton, Ohio

Thomas D. Rowe, Jr.
Professor
Duke Law School
Durham, North Carolina

Jacquelyn Sato
Author
Kentwood, Michigan

Kenneth Smith
History Teacher
Louisville Public Schools
Louisville, Ohio

Kenneth Wulff, Ph.D.
Teacher Dev. and Curriculum Studies
Kent State University
Canton, Ohio

I also wish to thank my sisters, Fae Koelker and Bou Walters, for contributing in numerous ways and encouraging the completion of this endeavor.

Library of Congress Catalog Card Number 87-50078
International Standard Book Number 0-942431-00-6

This book is dedicated to the memory of my father
who was old enough, and wise enough,
to love freedom
more than any other person I know.

This book was written to serve a dual purpose. When used as a picture book, it gives the young child some basic information about our Constitution. It may also be used as a guideline for presenting your own program about the Constitution.

Permission granted for use of the song AMERICA, from BEST LOVED SONGS OF THE AMERICAN PEOPLE, by Denes Agay, obtained from:
Doubleday & Company, Inc. Publishers
New York, New York 10167

Companion book also available:

MATERIALS FOR A CLASSROOM PRESENTATION OF THE CONSTITUTION OF THE UNITED STATES

Script, Props, and Activities
For Elementary School Children
Written and Illustrated by Janice Howes, M.Ed.

Teachers Publishing House
P. O. Box 9358
Canton, Ohio 44711

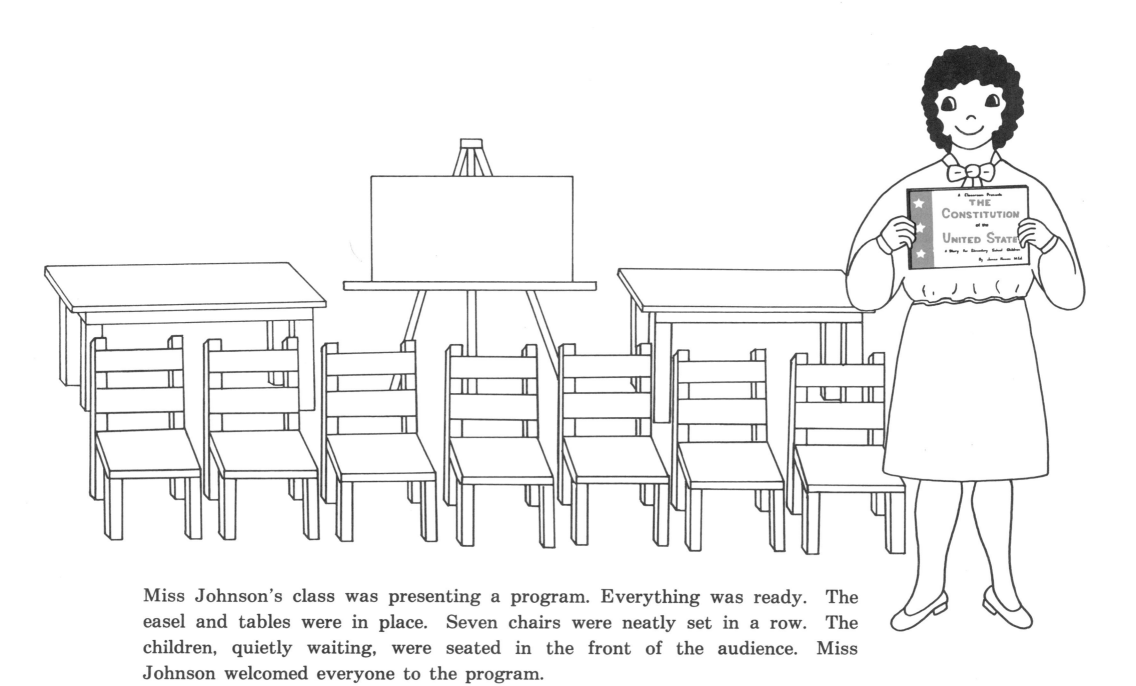

Miss Johnson's class was presenting a program. Everything was ready. The easel and tables were in place. Seven chairs were neatly set in a row. The children, quietly waiting, were seated in the front of the audience. Miss Johnson welcomed everyone to the program.

Johnny held the beautiful flag so that everyone could see it.

He said, "Will everyone please stand and say the Pledge of Allegiance to the flag."

When they were finished, everyone sat down, and Johnny put the flag on the table. The children began to tell the story of the Constitution of the United States.

About two hundred years ago, fifty-five men met together in Philadelphia to talk about writing a plan for the government of our new country. They called this plan the Constitution of the United States. George Washington was the president of that important meeting.

It was a big job to write the Constitution. The men at the meeting did not want our country to be ruled by a king. They wanted the people to have a part in our government. They had to think about what kinds of laws should be written. They had to think about the Indians, and about people who lived in other countries, too.

Sometimes the men were happy. Sometimes they were sad or angry, and then they would argue. Sometimes they were puzzled. But they were always thinking about what would be best for our country.

James Madison is often called the "Father of the Constitution". He did a lot of writing at the meeting.

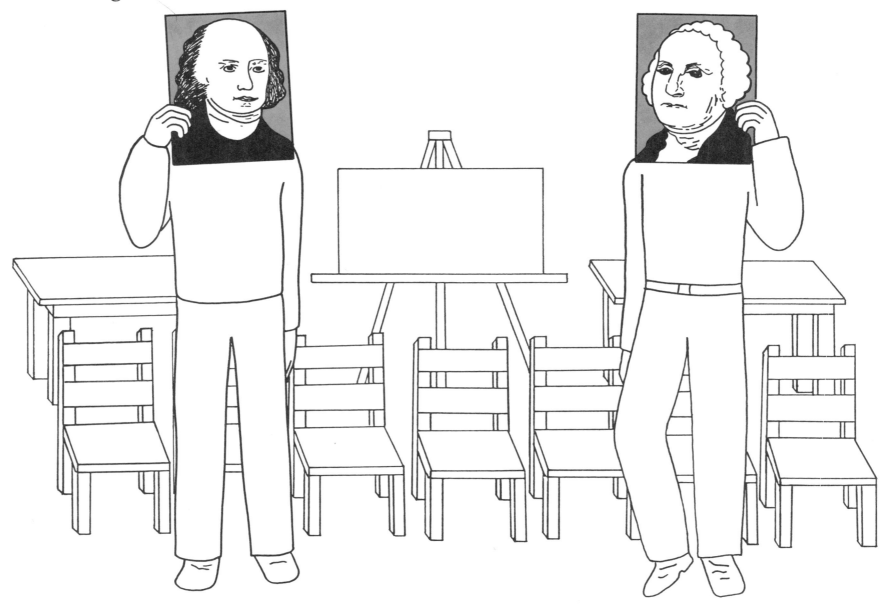

The fifty-five men who met together to write the Constitution came from many different states. It took them almost four months to write the Constitution.

The United States Constitution is the highest law of our country. It tells us how to organize our federal government. The federal government is the government of our whole country. The Constitution tells what our federal government is allowed to do.

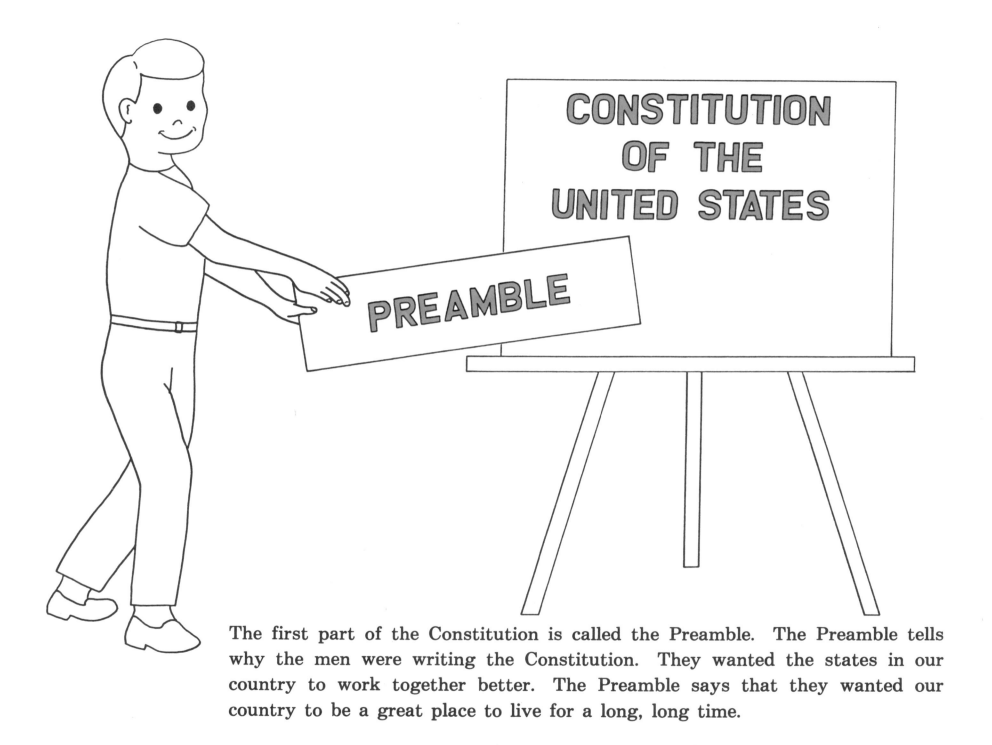

The first part of the Constitution is called the Preamble. The Preamble tells why the men were writing the Constitution. They wanted the states in our country to work together better. The Preamble says that they wanted our country to be a great place to live for a long, long time.

When the Constitution was first written it had seven parts which were called articles. The first three articles tell about the three branches of our government.

The first branch is Congress.

Article I says that our government has a Congress, with two parts, a Senate, and a House of Representatives.

When we vote we choose who we want for our Senators and Representatives. Congress makes the laws for our country.

The second branch is the President.

Article II says that our government has a President. Every four years we can vote for the person we want for President. The President and his helpers make sure that the laws are used to help the people, and that the people obey the laws. He also meets with leaders of other countries to talk about peace. He tells us about his work when he talks to us on television.

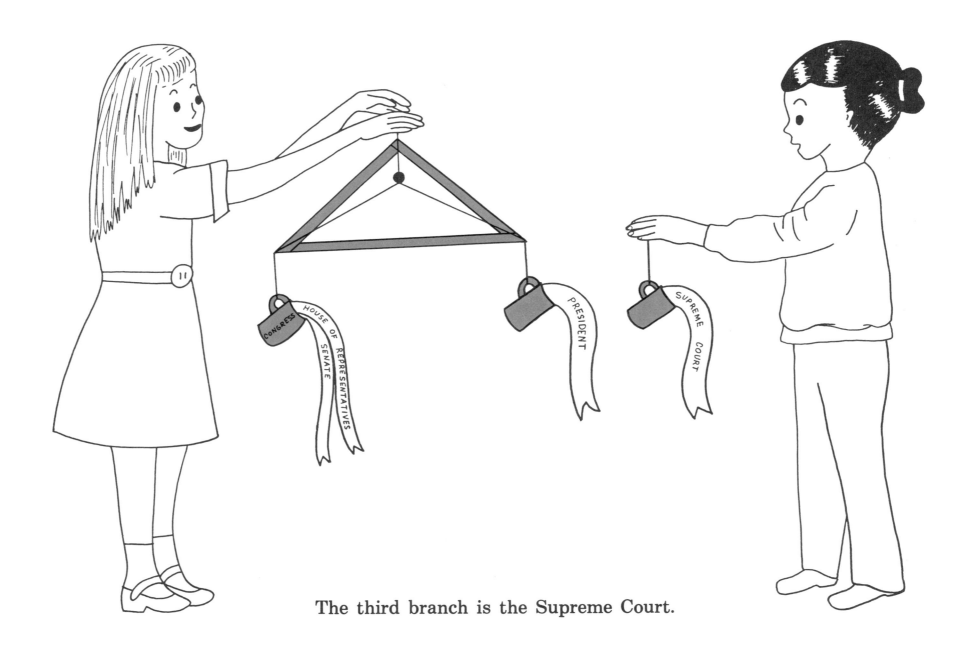

The third branch is the Supreme Court.

Article III says that our government has a Supreme Court. The nine justices of the Supreme Court explain the law. When people go to court because they disagree about something very important, the justices decide who is right according to the Constitution.

The three parts of our government — the Congress, the President, and the Supreme Court — must always do their jobs. Our government should be balanced to make sure that our people can live and be free and try to be happy.

Article IV tells some things that the states are allowed to do. A person can go to Florida, California, or any state, and still be safe and happy.

Article V says that the Constitution can be changed. It isn't easy to do this. Many states must agree that it should be changed. A change, or something that is added, is called an amendment.

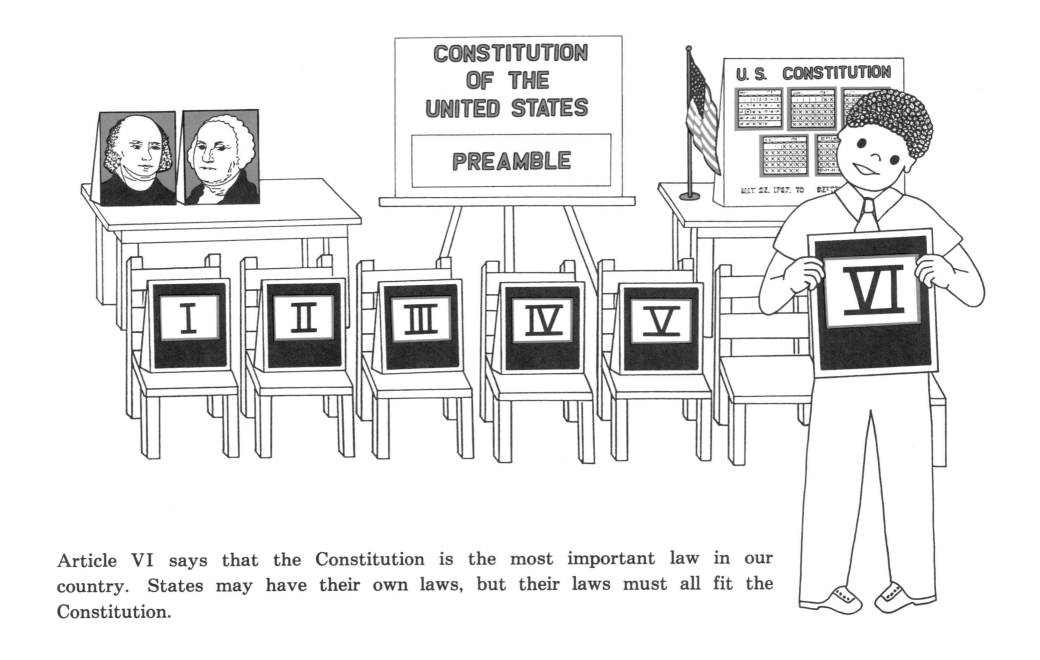

Article VI says that the Constitution is the most important law in our country. States may have their own laws, but their laws must all fit the Constitution.

Article VII says that before the Constitution could be used most of the states had to ratify it. They had to approve, or accept, the Constitution.

After the men finished writing this last article, they signed the Constitution. They signed their names because they thought the Constitution would make our country good and strong — a happy place to live. Thirteen men had gone home. Forty-two were still there, and thirty-nine of them signed the Constitution.

There were only thirteen states when the Constitution was signed. People in these states had to think and talk about the Constitution. They had to decide whether to ratify it or not. The Constitution became our new law when most of the states ratified it by voting "yes".

Twenty-six amendments have been added to the Constitution. The first ten amendments were added right away. They were called the Bill of Rights. They make sure that the government of our country does not treat us wrongly.

The Bill of Rights says that we have freedom to worship God. We may read the Bible and pray if we want to. We may go to any church we choose.

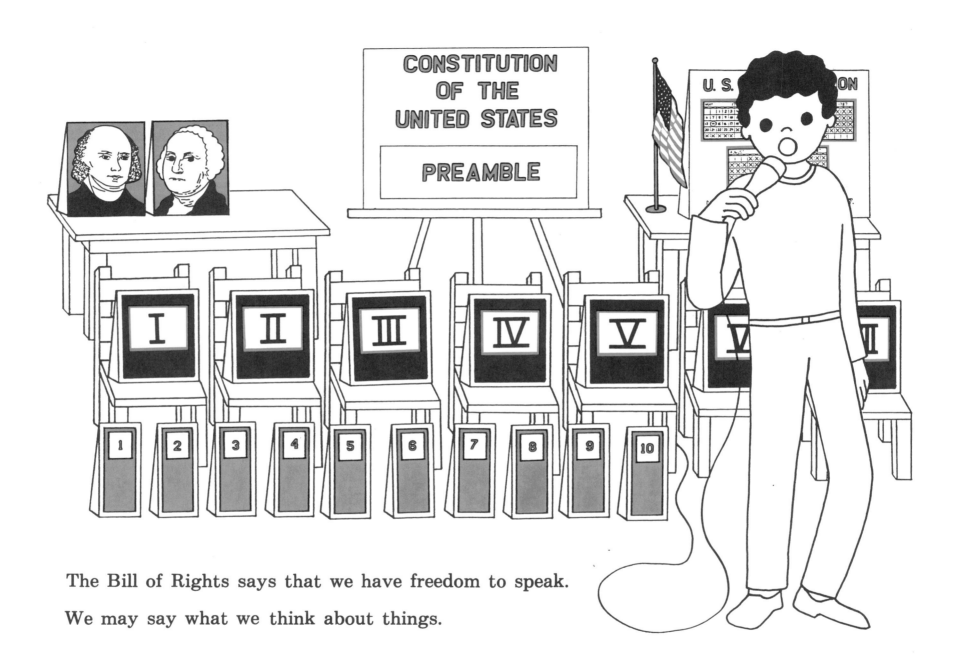

The Bill of Rights says that we have freedom to speak.

We may say what we think about things.

The Bill of Rights says that we have freedom to print the truth about things, and how we feel about them. We have freedom to read anything we choose.

The Bill of Rights says that the police can't take a person to jail without being fair. A person is allowed to tell his side of a story to a group of people called a jury. The jury listens and decides whether the person has broken the law or not.

After the Bill of Rights, more amendments were added. The 11th Amendment tells about lawsuits against states. The 12th Amendment tells how we choose our President and Vice-President.

Amendments 13, 14, and 15 were added after the Civil War ended, and after Abraham Lincoln was the President of the United States.

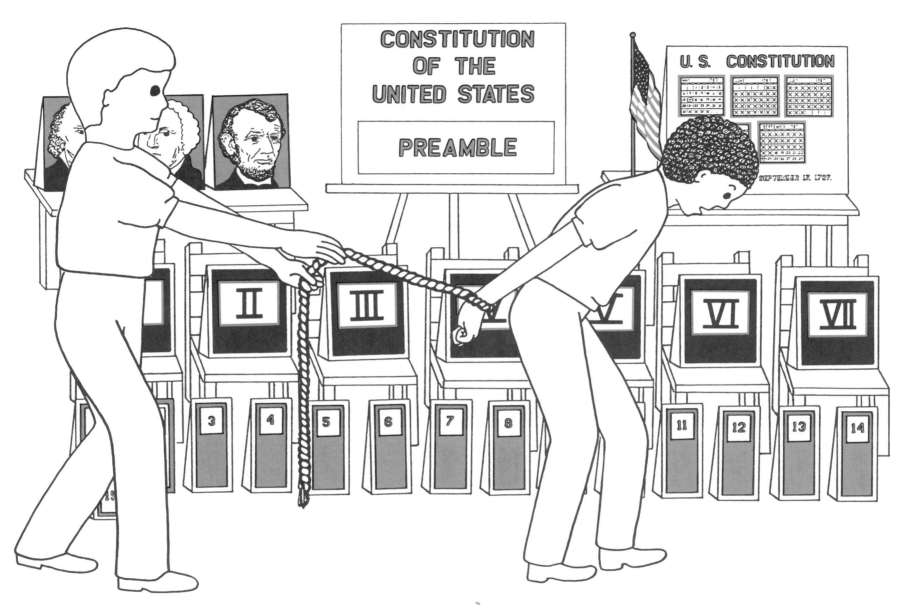

Before the 13th, 14th, and 15th Amendments there were many black slaves in the southern states.

These three amendments set the slaves free, made them citizens, and said that people may not be kept from voting because of the color of their skin. Many black children began to go to school for the first time.

People from other countries may come to the United States and become citizens. All citizens must be treated fairly.

The 16th Amendment says that the government of our country may have an income tax.

The 17th Amendment says that we may vote for Senators.

The 18th Amendment says that people are not allowed to make or sell beer or wine. That is called "Prohibition".

The 19th Amendment says that women may vote.

The 21st Amendment is about "Prohibition". It says that the 18th Amendment is not a law anymore, and that people may make or sell beer or wine if they want to. The 21st Amendment ended "Prohibition".

The 20th Amendment says that a new President or new Congressman may start working on his job earlier than before.

The 22nd Amendment says that no person may be chosen for President of the United States more than two times.

The 23rd Amendment says that the people in Washington D.C. (the capital of the United States) are allowed to vote for who they want for President.

The 24th Amendment says that voting is free. We don't have to pay tax money in order to vote.

The last amendment is number 26. It says that people may vote as soon as they are eighteen years old.

The 25th Amendment tells us what to do if something happens to the President and he can't finish his job. Then the Vice-President becomes the new President. It also tells us what to do if the Vice-President can't finish his job.

Someday, more amendments may be added to our Constitution. We have plenty of paper, and we can make changes if we need to.

The men who wrote our Constitution wanted the people in our country to live and be free and try to be happy. That's what we still want today. We must all work together to keep our country strong.

The Constitution of the United States is wonderful and very important! It is older than the constitution of any other country.

All the children marched to the front of the room with their flags. They sang "America" and it was beautiful!

The children in the class learned a lot about the Constitution. They were proud and happy to live in a free country. Aren't you glad you live in a country where you are an important part of the government?